LATE INTERMEDIATE LEVEL

Sonatina Humoresque

BY CHRISTOS TSITSAROS

CONTENTS

ISBN 978-1-4234-6885-1

7777 W. BLUEMOUND RD. P.O. BOX 13819 MILWAUKEE, WI 53213

In Australia Contact:
Hal Leonard Australia Pty. Ltd.
4 Lentara Court
Cheltenham, Victoria, 3192 Australia
Email: ausadmin@halleonard.com.au

Copyright © 2009 by HAL LEONARD CORPORATION
International Copyright Secured   All Rights Reserved

For all works contained herein:
Unauthorized copying, arranging, adapting, recording, Internet posting, public performance,
or other distribution of the printed music in this publication is an infringement of copyright.
Infringers are liable under the law.

Visit Hal Leonard Online at
www.halleonard.com

Sonatina Humoresque

I. Preambulum

By Christos Tsitsaros

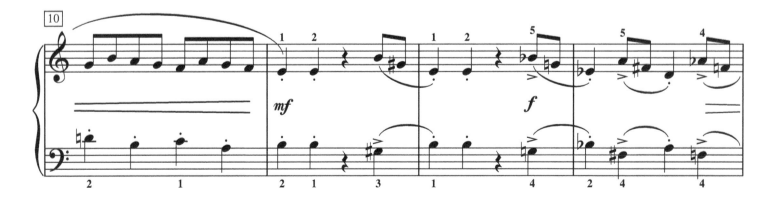

Copyright © 2009 by HAL LEONARD CORPORATION
International Copyright Secured   All Rights Reserved

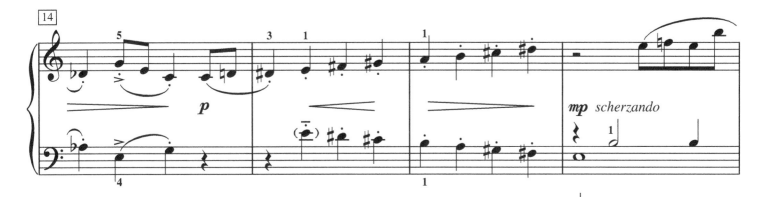

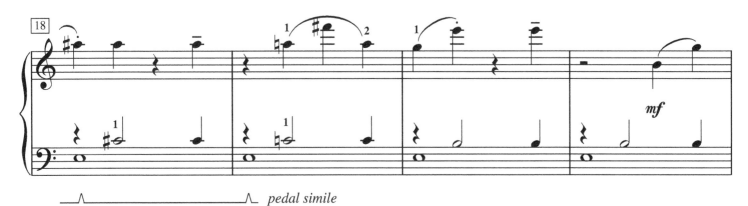

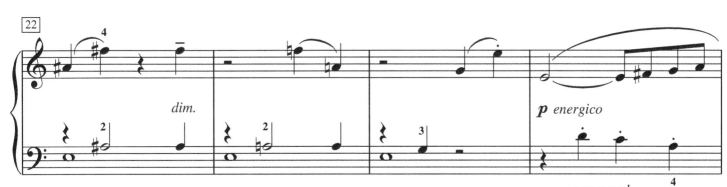

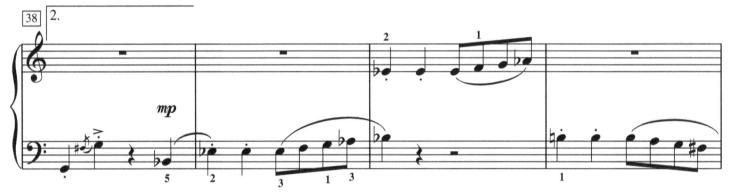

4

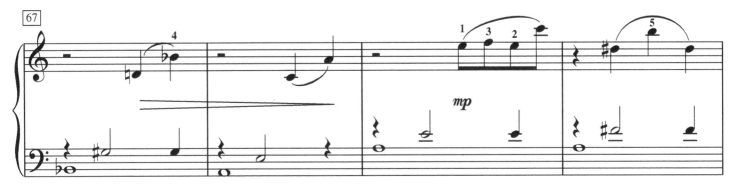

_⌄_ *simile ped.*

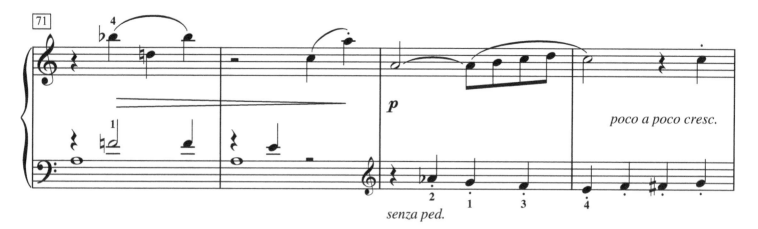

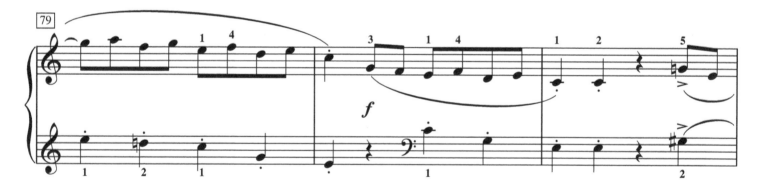

6

2'19"

II. Pastorale

Molto andante e espressivo (♩ = 80)

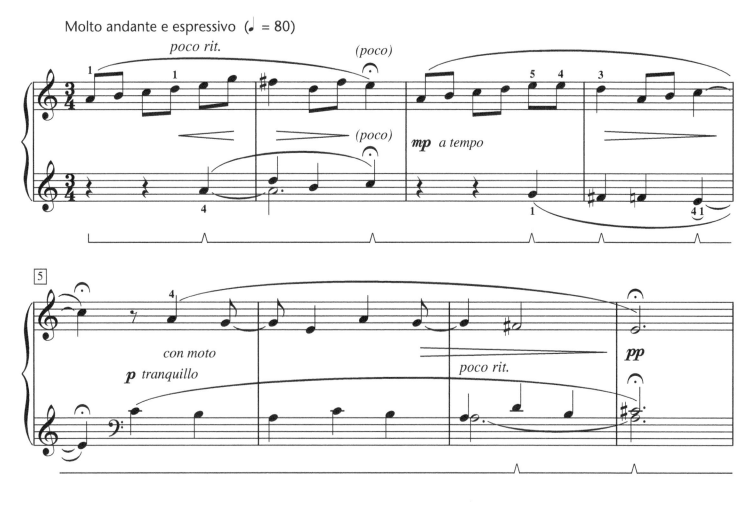

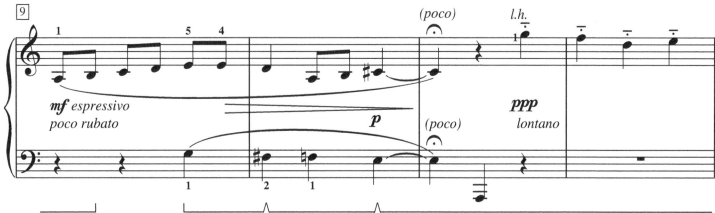

Copyright © 2009 by HAL LEONARD CORPORATION
International Copyright Secured   All Rights Reserved

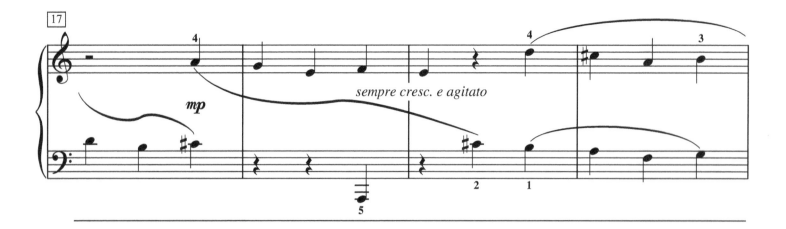

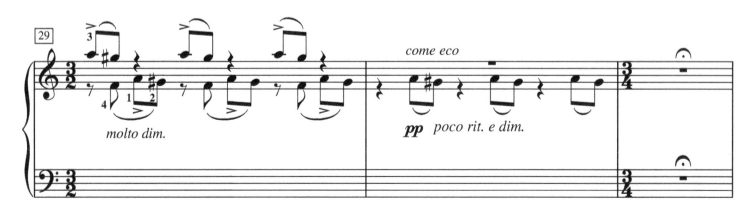

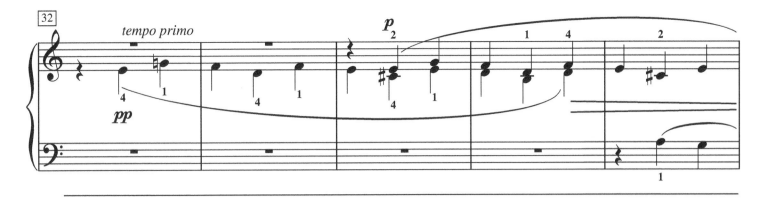

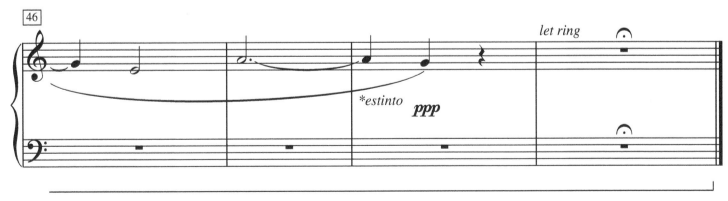

*extinguished

2'09"

9

III. Scherzo

Presto con spirito ($\quarternote\mathbf{.} = 108\text{-}112$)

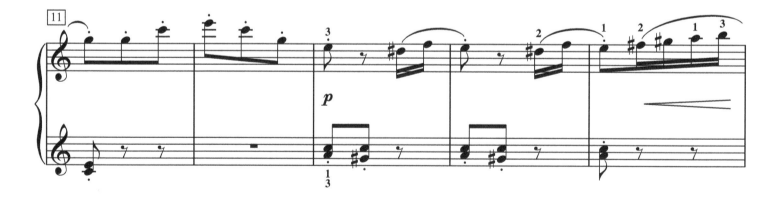

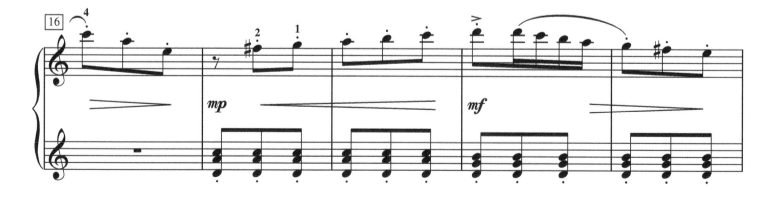

Copyright © 2009 by HAL LEONARD CORPORATION
International Copyright Secured   All Rights Reserved

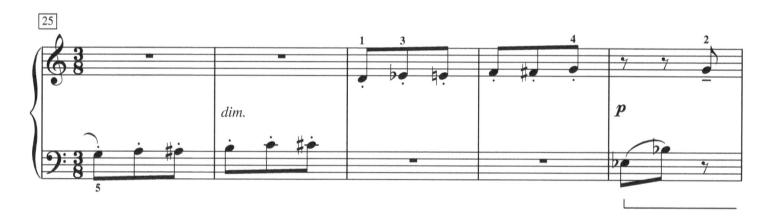

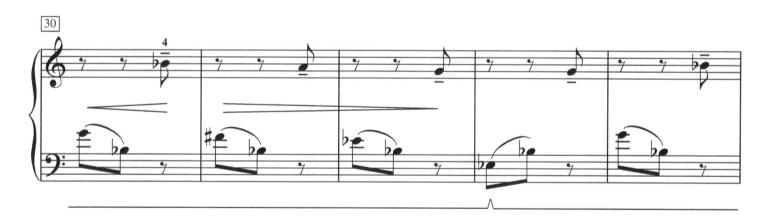

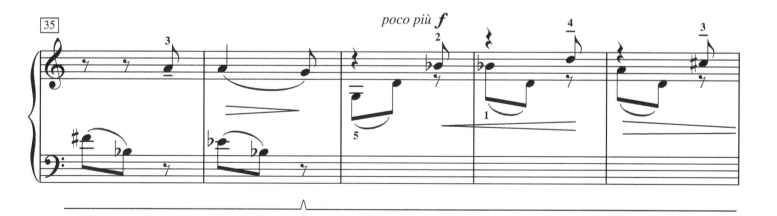

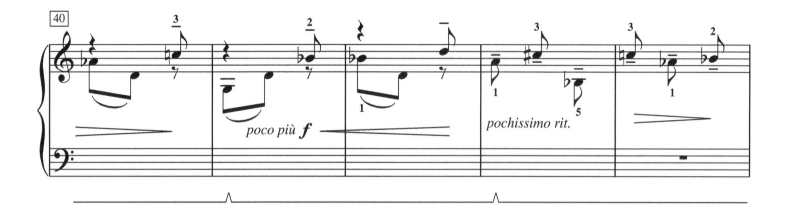

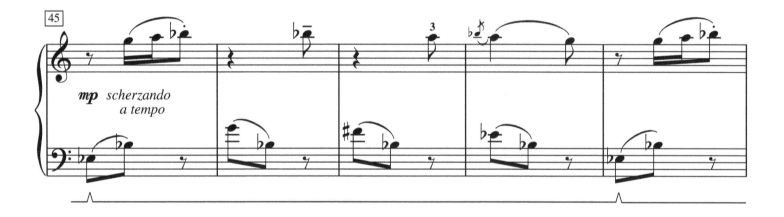

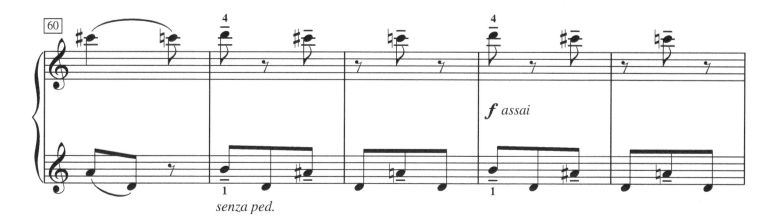

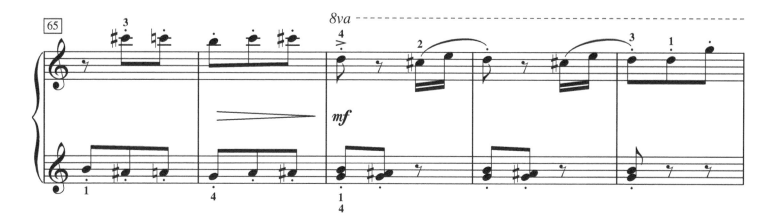

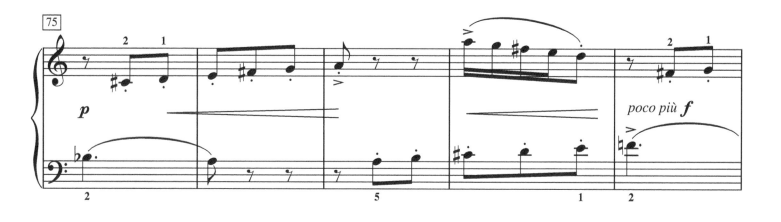

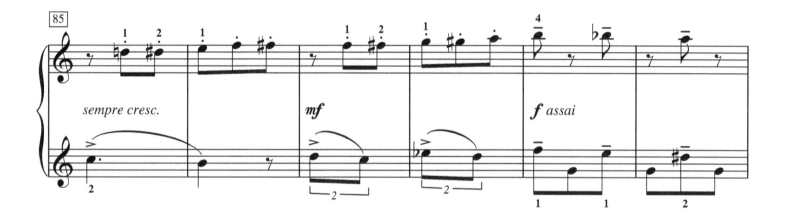

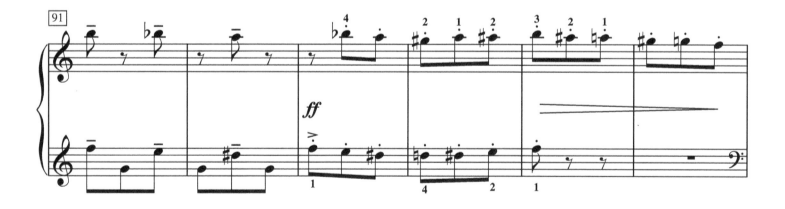

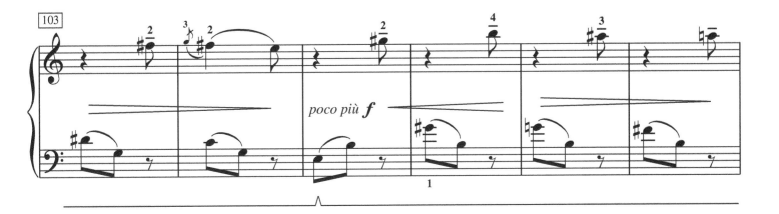

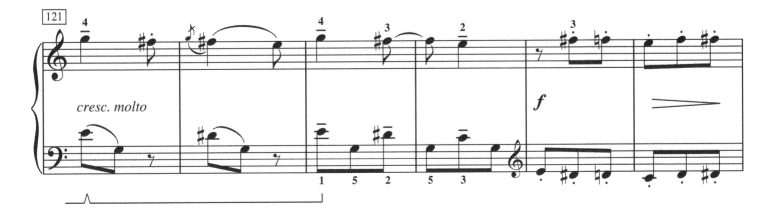

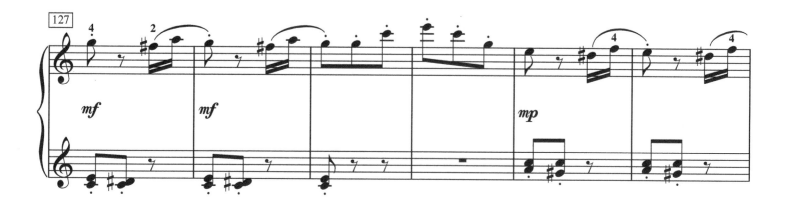

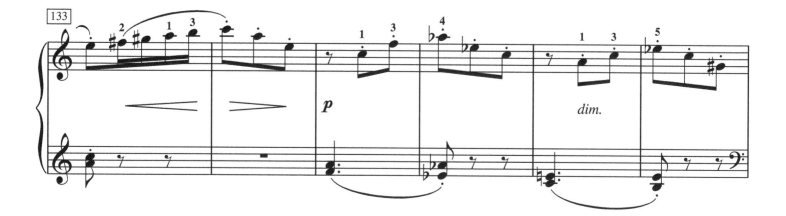

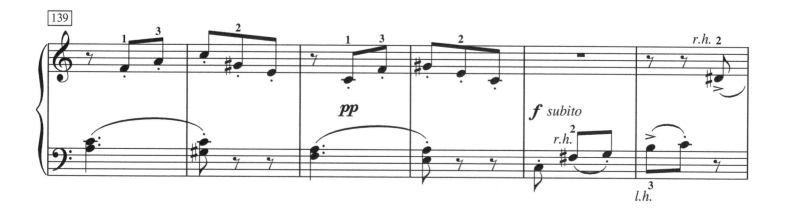

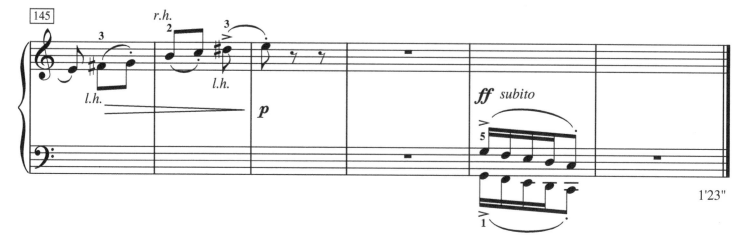

1'23"